Such Sweet Sorrow

Richard Bell

Such Sweet Sorrow

Such Sweet Sorrow
ISBN 978 1 76041 687 4
Copyright © Richard Bell 2019

First published 2019 by
GINNINDERRA PRESS
PO Box 3461 Port Adelaide 5015 Australia
www.ginninderrapress.com.au

Contents

Preface	7
On being told	9
Towards an unknown region	10
The bliss of ignorance	11
The depths of love	13
The mathematical curve of your life	14
Fake News: 13 July 2016	15
The perfect curve	16
When we last spoke	17
The comfort of others	19
And on the second last day	21
Last day	22
drae	23
The control of pain	25
Chromosome Eleven	28
What image springs to mind	30
Our history in your nightwear	31
They can go	32
My right hand	33
Walking together but alone	35
The grille between us	37
Holding ourselves within ourselves	38
The purple nightie	39
Space to think	40
The administrative side of death	42
Wish you were here	44
Do I miss you?	45
The house is colder since you left	46
Senses of loss	47
I loved the way you'd kill my jokes	49
Such sweet sorrow	50

Preface

In 1969, we decided to marry two days after we first kissed. Two weeks later, we married on the way to university, three weeks before the final exams. For the next forty-five years, we leisurely repented together. In 2014 Sue was diagnosed with a rare cancer. I wrote a few poems at the time, and I wrote some more in the last days of her life in December 2016. But most were written in the next eight months. To paraphrase Walt Whitman,

> I love another,
> now my love is no longer returned –
> yet out of this I have written these poems.

On being told

There is a point on the path of life
where the inevitability of death becomes real.
We were sort of at that point the evening
you came home and said you had cancer.

It was a winter's evening and darkening,
you walked straight past
the middle room where I was reading,
and into the kitchen space. I followed.
The downlights were on over the bench,
making it theatre.
You rolled a few words
along the stainless-steel top and
we slid our hips along it into a numb embrace.

A pancreatic neuro-endocrine tumour – metastases
in the liver, lymph nodes and bone, with
two, maybe two and a half years to live.

Maybe we were old enough, or too old, or maybe we
had been battered enough by health problems,
we took it calmly, held each other tight,
while you said, on being told this savage truth
you had cried out, 'I won't see my granddaughter grow up!'
and I could only wonder
at how you had managed to carry
this news home on the train
alone.

Towards an unknown region

Yesterday was not different
from today. A dark and empty night,
five dark hours of empty thoughts
rolled one into the other.
Last evening's words changed our lives
and today the empty grey skies
reflect my empty mind.

Where are we going?
When do we get there?
How do we move?
Why? I don't ask why,
it is enough that our life has changed.

Now we stumble blindly
along a new and different path
towards
an unknown region.

The bliss of ignorance

16 March 2000: 'large well-defined what appear to be almost water density foci within both lobes of the liver, the largest within the right lobe measuring 8 centimetres and within the left lobe 5.5 centimetres.'
11 October 2004: 'Sue has no evidence of MEN1 related endocrine tumours…'
11 August 2006: 'High-density lesion in segment 3 of the liver, ??complex cyst, ??malignancy.'
13 December 2007: 'In the posterior aspect of segment 3 of the liver is a relatively poorly-defined structure of high density. This could represent a complex cyst, although the possibility of malignancy cannot be entirely excluded.'
30 August 2012: 'Multiple hepatic cysts measuring up to 15 centimetres. Heterogeneous enhancing lesion within the left lobe of liver segment 3 with CT appearance favouring focal nodular hyperplasia.'
14 November 2014: 'Susan is a patient with a grade 2, FDG-avid, pancreatic neuroendocrine tumour on the background of MEN1. She is known to have disease in the liver as well as nodal involvement and multiple bony metastases.'

At first, we were incredulously angry.
How could they have missed it?
You confronted them, I rationalised that
your current treatments were not available at the time.

Now I know the treatments
were useless, some even less so,
and your life was not extended
beyond that estimate in the initial diagnosis.

And now I'm thinking the misdiagnoses
through those years was a hidden blessing,
eight years cocooned in ignorance –
not for us Coleridge's Ancient Mariner*

No, we luxuriated
in the bliss of ignorance.

* 'Like one, that on a lonesome road
Doth walk in fear and dread,
And having once turned round walks on,
And turns no more his head;
Because he knows, a frightful fiend
Doth close behind him tread.'

The depths of love

tragedy reveals
unknown depths of love

words are choked off
and squeezed into tears

in this silence
red-rimmed eyes
exchange glances

which speak more to love
than words could ever do.

The mathematical curve of your life

The pre-dawn light
fills the window
at the end of the bed
and silhouettes the curve
that is your hip under blankets

what is the area under this curve?
your life?

in younger days
estimated in theory
by integrating to infinity.

Now there's a finite limit:
our life is bounded by a couple of years,

we estimate the area
by cautious quadrature,
delineating life
by the finite elements
of love
pleasure
and pain.

Fake News: 13 July 2016

A consultant told you
'Good news! The treatment is working.
Make plans for an overseas trip
at the end of the year.'
You came home elated.
'I think I was a bit manic,' you said.
We went to the local for a celebratory drink.
I, either (as usual) overly enthusiastic,
or desperate – not looking too closely,
began making plans, and you,
even as we sat on the leather couches
in front of the low fire sipping our beer,
slowly retreated from your optimism
– though to be fair, my enthusiasm
for any plan of a trip always
had such an effect on you.

But now, a year on, looking back at the dates
on your painkiller medication, I think
you were listening to your body
and thinking, 'No.'

So it turned out to be. He was wrong.
You were right. Your only trip
was across that last river,
and I am still paying the ferryman.

The perfect curve

With just two or three months left in our life,
each morning after a cautious embrace
you would lie on your back looking up
at nothing. You would smile a little
as I softly kissed your shoulder
and put my arm across your hips,
my right hand on your left hip socket
that would never need replacing and
the inside of my wrist perfectly curved over
that mound between your hips. Each time
I gave you just enough energy to roll
past my embrace and slowly out of bed.
One more day begun.

When we last spoke

A Christmas card, based on a Japanese woodblock print:
three young girls making a snow rabbit
on a moonlit winter's night.
Sent by an old friend, rarely met
and consequently, full of the year's news.
You looked at it in puzzlement and slowly tried
to read inside. I sat beside the bed and
held your warm but weak hand in mine as
you struggled to comprehend the lines
that yesterday you had simply been too tired to read.
'Zoë?' you asked, not so much of me, but of your memory.
'Sandra's daughter – the same age as Alice,' I said.
Alice, your daughter, was still memory-accessible,
though Sandra was a line-ball decision.

We went through the card,
line by line, word by word, until
exhausted, you could take no more
and slumped back on your pillows while
I put the card back on the bedside table.
That was the last time we spoke together.

In the afternoon we were strangers,
though our faces each reminded the other
of who we might have been, which led to slight smiles,
the sort that people sometimes direct at others
who they think they might know.

And at 4 p.m. the registrar said, 'It's only days until the end.'
On Monday, it had been hinted months were possible,
on Wednesday, weeks were predicted.

Now Friday, days.
This time they got it right.

The comfort of others

Saturday, and they've moved you
to a bigger room with a window wall
but your eyes are unseeing now
and your bed lies upon the floor
for safety's sake – they wouldn't want you
to fall out of bed in your agitation
– you might hurt yourself! And
your hand, now on automatic agitation pilot,
reaches out vaguely. (My God, how hard this is to write!)

The weeping cleaner, the girl now woman,
who has come fortnightly for twenty years,
brings her Greek orthodox priest and acolyte
to pray for you on one knee. It doesn't do
much for you, but she leaves
revitalised. My brother reads you
D.H. Lawrence's 'Ship of Death', and though
you turn a deaf ear, he leaves comforted.

And there is a procession of other visitors. Some
need to make contact, fall upon your wandering hand
as a sign, a reaching out they need. While others,

discomforted, stand around awkwardly,
shocked, try for small talk and fail.
'But this has been all so quick,' they cry.
And there are flowers of comfort: formal arrays from florists,
best blooms from front gardens,
and small informal posies.

Finally, the room is empty and quiet.
You look as comfortable as you have looked
all day: you haven't moved, with shallow breathing
and the gentlest plucking at your bedclothes.

And on the second last day

How long must
you lie there –
empty eyes staring
waiting for the ferryman
waiting for Charon
to carry you out of this life
across the Styx.

What lies on the other side?
The myth said Heaven or Hell –

I think it's both:
your empty body
with its traitorous cells,
will be burned;
but the spirit of your life will live on

in other's memories.
Some will fade
faster than others, some
will burn on in the tears
of dreamless dark nights, and

some memories will bring a simple smile
that leaves other passengers on the 8.15
wondering.

Last day

It sounds like death
is near now
rasping gasps
of breath drag air
uselessly
into your failing body.

The nurses have swept the hair off your face
your mouth is fixed wide open
and your colourless eyes just stare –
death has no time
for modesty or looks.

A different story
when it comes
to humiliating body and mind:
then death
has all the time in the world.

A drug stops
the rasping noise.

In the silence
I watch the faltering
rise and fall of your bed covers.

Then stillness.
Time stops.

I lay the warm back of my hand
against your cold cheek.
You have gone.

drae

We call them side effects
but the correct term
is drug related adverse events
which I've shortened to drae,
as it has a Scottish feel to it,
and you liked Scottish poetry.

Cancer poems are full of drae,
indeed, cancer treatment is full of drae.
There are two kinds,
internal, such as pain or nausea
that you could hide, and external,
changes to your appearance that
signalled to others 'I'm in treatment.'
The latter you liked less.

Such as the frizzy hair
that came along with the first drug
though we were never sure whether
it might have been just due to old age,
– but when the drug was stopped
(it didn't work) the frizziness went away
as did the stained nails.

The next treatment
was chemotherapy, an approach
with a monster drae reputation, but no,
no one could see any difference in you,
the red cell deficiency and exhaustion
were invisible, and the nausea didn't exist –
other 'powerful anti-nausea' drugs were used,
of course, they too had their drae: sleeplessness
and nightmares – but only I saw those.

the final treatment,
peptide-receptor-radionuclide-therapy,
brought drae: unseen platelets wiped out,
pain – treated with drugs that brought along
their own drae of constipation and nausea,

and you lost some hair,
(your worst nightmare all along)
but not enough for me to participate
in that cancer-spousal poetry de rigueur moment
of cutting off your remaining hair, no,
Ben on Toorak Road could carefully
hide the loss.

And at the end, there were obvious signs,
yellow skin, agitated movement, unconsciousness
but these were crae not drae.

The control of pain

There was always a medical confidence
about managing pain – you just had to get
the drug and dose matched to the level of pain,
(okay it might take a couple of days)
but the pain would be controlled –
or not – as it turned out to be.

But first there was the reason:
was this pain from tumours,
or from treatment?
We always hoped it was the latter,
since that would end sometime –
but cancer pain that could go on
and on until the end, a possibility
we kept from ourselves.

But the pains of the tumours,
like the tumours themselves, grow;
and the painkillers were always
playing catch-up. This much I know.

You started with Panadol, quickly
added codeine, 10, 15, 30 milligrams,
switched to oxycodone in another month,
that held six weeks (well nearly),
then changed tack.

Serious pain management,
we learned, is two-pronged:
there is a base continuous drug,
and a second 'breakthrough'
one to check odd flare-ups of pain.
Pain management now was more complex –
I started keeping records of what and when.

We started with one beginning with 'T',
maybe targin or tramadol, as base, and
oxycodone as breakthrough
 – it didn't work, the pain
was getting away again, so
after a visit to emergency
there was a shift to oxycontin as base
 – which also didn't work
after a week or two.

Then it was the big one, fentanyl,
ten times (or 100) more powerful than morphine
(depending on the sensationalism of the news report)
stepping up quickly through 25, 37,
to 50 micrograms per hour
with morphine sulphate as breakthrough.
It lasted ten days.

By now they were saying
take the breakthrough whenever.
No longer had you to ask:
'Can I have another painkiller yet?'

The final shot was one more switch
to a continuous pump of a less powerful drug
'sometimes a change in drug works –
it overcomes the habituation of the other'.

It worked for a few days,
but as the new drug stopped the pain (maybe),
the cancer stopped everything else.

Pain controlled.

Chromosome Eleven

Lying there together
in post-coital darkness
morning, noon, or night,
our minds flipped channels
between the mild anxiety
of what we might have just done,
or the silly grins recalling the ecstasy
of what we had just done.

While my army of spermatozoa
was lolling about your tubes, job done,
rubbing shoulders with the cells
of uterine walls, you'd think
they might have noticed something:
'Hey sweetie, your chromosome eleven
is missing some postcodes. Can we help?
Chummy here won't need his, let us
put them in your place.'
But no, the selfish bastards
just went on working their way
through their six-packs of lager
until it was time to be discharged,
wiped away on a tissue.

'Typical' is what you'd have said
if you had known 'It's what I would have expected
from your side of the family.'

But you didn't.
And now we don't. We aren't.

And I just get to replay memories
such as this. As often as I like.

What image springs to mind

What image springs to mind
when I say your name?
Before your death, it was the time I saw you last,
Now, I just don't know.

Memories jostle for attention
as I think of you. Five months
later they are older ones
that follow photographs: sometimes
I think the blurred ones best –
arousing feelings while
leaving space for the interpretation of situations,
at other times, the clearly focused
suit me more – the sharp blue of your eyes,
the precise line of your smile
that delineates a moment to stop my heart.

I think I see you as I need to see you
a kaleidoscope of fragments, no single image will do,
portraits of the roles you played and play in my life –
confidante, critic, lover, mother, and wife.

Our history in your nightwear

your nightwear fashions
went in phases:

the first night we shared a bed
it was short in orange gingham
(I think your mother made it)
with lacy knickers –
a temporary phase

then when we moved to colder Melbourne
there was the long fuzzy nylon
uncertain phase
designed in part I think
to kill lust (it did).

but for most of our nights together
it was just an old tee-shirt
in your mind, a balance between decorum and freedom,
in mine, a quasi-nightie phase of possibilities.

And naked was for love
or hot Perth nights (or both):
I think of it longingly
as the 'anticipation of global warming' phase.

In the end though,
it was half a dozen more carefully chosen
modest (but attractive) nighties
frequently washed,
that mostly served to soak up sweat.
These were the nightgowns of approaching death.

They can go

How can I throw these things out?
These books. These boxes of her books,
they can go, no, not those,
I'm keeping them to read
some day.
This dozen balls of wool, needles, there must be
five or six dozen pairs in this bag, this
half-finished red something – I can't find
the pattern to give me a clue. Don't I
know someone who knits? No. Like sewing
it's dying. Speaking of which (sewing not dying)
there are also these lengths of material waiting
on patterns (yes, there's at least one box of those)
to be turned into little dresses or shirts –
they now can go, too.

Am I losing her in all this? I don't think so.
Her things I mean to keep
are the keepsakes that are part of me.
I remember, some years after my father died
I threw an old overnight bag out and was shocked
to burst into tears. He had bought it for me long ago.
So, I expect I'll know, my tears will tell me,
if I throw the wrong things out.

As for these pink bowls,
I never liked them – they can go.

My right hand

The memory of her body
is best contained
in my right hand. Mornings,
I would roll in bed towards her,
she half asleep, sometimes half-awake in pain,
and remind myself
of her physical presence:

a tense body meant pain
and I would helplessly cup
her shoulder in my hand,
and stroke her shoulder blade
slowly with my thumb,
or run my hand slowly down her arm
to hold her cold hand.

or run my hand slowly down her arm
to hold her cold hand.

But relaxed, then I'd run my hand
tentatively along the upper rim
of her rolled away hip,
hips only just wide enough
for childbearing (two).
My hand would feel
it's on wedlock edge
and slide down
along the outside of her cool thigh
to pause at her crook'd knee:

Sometimes she'd move her hips
back, a little closer to mine, and
emboldened, my hand would move,
slide around the tender waist of her problems
to pause at her navel, then either
ripple up her sharper ribs
to cup her warm left breast,
or slide down and run my fingers
along the cleft that lay
beneath her soft curling hair –
until she would take my hand firmly,
kiss the fingers, then safely park it
in the unexcitable space
between her breasts,
and press us together
in one more embrace.

My right hand remembers
all of this.

Walking together but alone

'I like to be by myself often – especially to walk with my thoughts along a quieting beach' – diary, Wednesday 16 July 1969

You appeared to be the always social one in the family.
But this was not true, there were times and a place
in which you sought solitude; on a beach
with me, always a beach, and always
with a headland in the distance.
I was the only one who saw you alone,
and though we walked together we walked
alone, each lost in our thoughts, but always with
an eye for where the other was.

I lost count of the number of times
we walked West Beach at Robe:
where sharp rocks gave way
to white hot sand and the cold wind, that screamed
across from the Bight, shredded the tops
of waves, to whip up the beach, while
you, daringly, skirted the foaming edge of
the undisciplined waves that broke irregularly,
your pants rolled just high enough (usually).

Or just after the diagnosis, (a break because we could)
east of Separation Creek on a late winter's beach,
you strode out across the wet flat sand
alone with your thoughts of the future. What future?

In the end, death was just another headland
to move towards, and in that last walk
along the edge of the waves of pain
that too often wrapped around your waist,
you were likewise alone; I was there, helplessly
holding your cold hand to no effect,
and you went on to that last beach ending
painfully alone.

The grille between us

'Driven against the grate of a mortal life'*
I feel the rusty bars against my cheek
as I strain to look through, my shoulder
still hurts from when I banged up against it
months ago, and now the lower corner
is digging into my pelvis, reminding me
of my empty bed.

I'd be better backed up against this grille,
arms outstretched, bound to the edges
with the barbed wire of others' sympathy:
crucified thus, I could no longer look to the past,
and be freed to weep
not for what was,
but for what was not.

* opening line taken from a Sharon Olds poem, 'The Pain of It'

Holding ourselves within ourselves

I had forgotten,
how all those years ago
I held myself within myself,
and how you, with a wicked smile,
would bait me, tease me
like a dancing bear, with words
that might promise something more
should I decide to lower my defences,
speak from myself, reveal my feelings.

In much later years, you no longer sought
the hidden me. I had nothing left to hide
and nothing to defend,
and I, I became lost for words, as
we moved into that uncomfortable state
of older age where nothing worked as before,
we both became within ourselves,
destined for what? I do not care to think.

But then the cancer came.
The wheel turned in a clumsy metaphor
and we were back where we began:
Again, I found your beauty intoxicating,
but you, well, my jokes no longer seemed
quite as funny. Still,
we managed to stumble together
to the end. Without not within,
Being ourselves, being each other.

And now, beside the myself
that I hold within myself,
I also hold your self – tightly.

The purple nightie

Your last nighties
were the first clothes to go
after you went –
but still I remember them

especially the long discreet
purple one
that held tight to your body
going around the curves.

Tonight, the memory reminded me
of the old purple cow poem,
so, on my mind I wrote

'I never liked a purple nightie,
it always makes me cough,
if I should see you wearing one
I'd have to take it off.'

and I could see you mutter
'In your dreams' or 'You wish'
and purse your lips

trying not to smile.

Space to think

With just six days
left in your life,
finally a doctor asks
'What do you want
from your treatment?'
Space to think, you say,
space for yourself, although,
even as you say this,
you struggle to find those words.

There'd been no such space
in treatments, nor had
anybody thought to ask.
Six months on a drug trial,
there was a gap then – but we took it
overseas to visit family and friends,
time not to be wasted in thinking;
next, eight months in chemotherapy
(fortnight on, fortnight off),
three months in radiotherapy
and (nearly) four months just in pain.

Somewhere in all that
you stole some space to think.
But you thought of 'us' not 'yourself',
you left journals and poems for me to find
on your bookshelf,
and a silver box on a high shelf upstairs
marked 'Us' that held all our letters,
postcards, and yes, more poems.

Now I have your space to think.
And all I can think of is you.

The administrative side of death

The administrative side of death
does not attract the attention of poets.
Impersonal, remote, and objective,
seemingly with no trigger for emotion.

For example, as autumn leaves, with no effort on my part
some of your plastic will wither
and die at their expiry date, falling into the bin
in a colourful shower. Buson
would knock up a quick haiku at this point.

Changing things in your name to mine is not so hard,
some accounts, and importantly your mobile phone –
but the only message from the days of you is from the vet
'It's time for Livia's anti cats AIDs injection.'

Events like this only take time – and some fortitude
in lasting out the mindless music while I wait
for the 'next available person' to deal with my routine task.

But in changing things in both our names to just mine,
Emotions ambush me. Suddenly I see
that we, that us, have become just I, and me.
A simple signature and we are lost.
Part of me has always been an 'us'. 'We'
had shaped the way I see the world – I'm sure
it was the same for you. But now
'S.J. & R.C. Bell' is just 'Richard Bell'. The house is mine,
not ours, the insurance, the rates notice and so on, also.

I sometimes feel I have stolen these from us,
and like Prometheus, who stole fire from the gods,
my liver is eaten daily by eagles in punishment,
though in this day and age, that translates
to simply drinking too much.

Wish you were here

'Wish you were here':
It's the sort of insincere remark
we put on postcards when we're somewhere
'gorgeous' or 'exciting', and we know
the other would 'just love it'.

But you and I wrote it to each other
often enough in enforced absences:
'wish you were here' meant 'I wish you were here'
with no thought for where we were
or why, just that it had clearly been a mistake
to part, and just as clearly, I missed you
and you missed me and how long would it be
before such a wish could be granted?
Of course, we only said those words
knowing such a parting was temporary –
togetherness would be restored
– and never a moment too soon.

Now there is an endless absence
there is no point to wishing you were here
(besides you would hate the cold
and the electricity prices would outrage you)
and instead I'm forced to wish that my memories
will not fade away.

(Wish you were here, though.)

Do I miss you?

Though you are not here,
it sometimes feels, it sometimes is,
for me, as though you are.

When I wake
in the less than half light
of a nearing winter's dawn,
there's a mound under the bedclothes
that, for less than a split second,
is you, lying beside me, but then
it turns out to be
what used to be your pillow,
dislodged by my uneasy sleep,
or the cat, pretending to be you, but
fooling no one (except me, momentarily).
And across the table at dinner, there's
the occasional momentary hallucination,
you're there – but no you're not,
though I can write down what you said
(after all these years).

Of course, I cheat in all this. I plant
significant photos of you at strategic points
around the house where I am prone to pause,
(oddly, photos mostly of you with the children
– you show up well in those) and reflect;
and re-read, with undiminished wonder,
the accounts we gave of ourselves and each other
in seemingly endless letters, poems, and postcards.

How can I miss you in all this?

The house is colder since you left

The house is colder since you left.
Now I add an extra jumper,
and a knee rug within reach, to save
heating up a whole room for just one.
– but I don't think that's the answer.

It's true it's winter, but hey,
there's global warming and spring is on its way
besides, there've been other winters
(one a year as I recall).

I could say it's all in the mind – but that's no explanation.
Is it then, in an eastern philosophical moment,
that I am the yin of coldness, and you were the yang of warmth?
Or is it that we were two cold hard things, like flint and steel,
that together struck a spark? Or was it, and I like this one,
that heat comes from friction (we had plenty of that),
one body rubbing up against the other
producing amongst other things children,
but in any case, warmth?

No, I'm afraid I'm driven to the occult
to explain this phenomenon:
The presence of ghosts is well-known to be signalled
by a drop in temperature:
I think you haunt this house –
you certainly haunt my mind.

Senses of loss

The senses in which I've lost you:
Well, there's visual for a start,
I no longer see you – except
in memories, in dreams, and
in countless photographs
strewn around the house.

In taste? No that is gone, though
I remember the slight salty taste of a kiss
on your warm shoulder. There never was
the taste of a kiss between us, that was all
touch (piqued sometimes by a sense of urgency)
– only memories there.

Smell? I can still pass your last slim bottle
of Laura Biagiotti under my nose
and pick up your scent, as you, last thing
before leaving the house, would always
go through the scent ritual:
spray a little on the inside of your left wrist,
wipe that wrist on the inside of the right,
and press both to your neck
beneath those perfect ears.

Hearing? I still hear echoes of your words
in my memories. When that fails I dial
a certain number to hear you say,
'Hi. You've called Sue and Richard Bell.
We can't take your call right now but
if you leave your name and number
we'll get back to you.'

And that's what I do. I get back to you
as often as I can – or even all the time.

I loved the way you'd kill my jokes

When my email told those who knew you,
you had died, there were some responses
that surprised me. I told my daughter
'They say your mother had a sense of humour'
and we would look at each other, mystified.

There was the time in Bologna (4 a.m.)
when an earthquake woke us, shaking the *letto matrimoniale*,
I said, 'And did the earth move for you too, darling?'
and you snapped, 'Don't be silly. It's an earthquake.'

Or later, when the drug-induced night terrors
threw you out of bed and your hands took the blow –
'My hands don't work' you said next morning so I replied
'Let's turn all the lights on – many lights make hands work.'
You looked at me. 'You're just like your father,' you said.

Later I found your saved cache of his letters to us,
written between our marriage and his death,
and yes, he had that way with words,
but your rejoinders turned jokes into theatre,
a two-handed comedy sketch:
I would still be smiling at your lines
days later – even now.

I loved the way you'd kill my jokes.

Such sweet sorrow

Parting? I don't know that we did,
it always seemed there would be
one more tomorrow, or an after lunch,
and never a point at which we could say
goodbye, *ciao*, or *auf wiedersehen* (you had all those languages).

No, there was an unseen atrophy
of communication while we were busy
fighting a rearguard action against pain.
Yes, we were on that darkling plain swept
with nausea and agitation, confused
about who we were and where we were at,
and may have missed the chance to say – what?

Or did we? Were words really our way?
What could we say that we hadn't said
in other ways, and so many times?

And you had quietly mustered an army
of memorabilia in reserve, anonymously
stacked on shelves or stored in a box
marked 'Us', to carry me through
what we both knew was the eventual parting.

For my part, I had winnowed out photographs
of you, of us, from the chaff of endless snaps
of where we had been and when or why,
views that had somehow lost their beauty.

Now I am left with just these: pictures, postcards,
poems, diaries, notes, and letters, both love and day-to-day.
From this I sometimes reconstruct the life that was us,
but each time the ending is one more parting,
and always of such sweet sorrow.

www.ingramcontent.com/pod-product-compliance
Lightning Source LLC
Chambersburg PA
CBHW062205100526
44589CB00014B/1965